SCORING THE SILENT FILM

SCORING THE SILENT FILM

poems

Keith Montesano

Dream Horse Press
Aptos, California

Dream Horse Press
Post Office Box 2080, Aptos, California 95001-2080

Scoring the Silent Film Copyright © 2013 Keith Montesano

Printed in the United States of America
Published in 2013 by Dream Horse Press

ISBN 978-1-935716-29-7

Cover artwork:

Film Noir #1
by Megi Rome

www.megiromeart.com

For my wife, Jessica. I can't thank you enough.

CONTENTS

What We Stare into is the Black Heart of Our Lives

What We Ask for Can Never Be Granted

What We Hope Will Never Find Us

What We Stare into is the Black Heart of Our Lives

THE AUTHOR AS MAN WHO HOLDS THE OTHER MOVIE CAMERA IN *THE BRIDGE*

After the documentary film by Eric Steel

Before he swan dives off the railing & the camera
      can't follow until the splash, we're left wondering
what happens to each person before they die: sharks
      to blood, burst kidneys, ribs that crack & rip through
the heart & ruptured liver. Too often no one's found,
      & the bones remain beneath skin as the body takes
its destined path. But is beauty sacrificed for the absent
      suicide barrier? The fog lifting to shroud our vision
before the man who throws his three year-old daughter
      & then follows? There's the fourteen year-old girl
who read Geo Stone's now out-of-print manual on suicide,
      who left a note for her mother on a computer, took a cab
a hundred miles before she jumped. The list is too long,
      & this camera can't follow the velocity of each
as few hesitate, some with arms behind them gripping rails,
      some talking on cell phones the moment before, leaving
wallets, backpacks, sandwich bags housing sentence-long
      scrawl. & again each splash: nearly silent, like a child
dropping a brick from that height, & mostly no one sees
      anything, or they ignore it & walk away, as I imagine
I would too, since my strength wouldn't be enough
      to pull someone up, when I'd be left with the last
thought of their eyes into mine, before every cinematic
      zoom & close-up, hands latticed & slipping: the fall
endless for me, just four to seven seconds for the rest.

THE AUTHOR AS MAN WHO SEES THE MECHANIC GET TRAPPED BETWEEN THE CAR AND THE WALL IN *VACANCY*

After the film by Nimrod Antal

When man becomes heart palpitations, drowned, stilled
        in greased hotel lights, too many bulbs out, caught between
the loose shred of skinned existence, its break, its shred
        & faulty mechanics: that's when we see our lives in play.
Someone should have a camera. The wind just mosquitoes,
        strident buzzing in the ear, prick & blood-suck as victory
before one swat, before we're covered with ours, the transport
        of others. The car was a battering ram, the mechanic there
& then not there, all in a matter of seconds. I am witness
        & to blame. I am the one who does nothing. To watch
& to wait, the weeds now swaying, ditch dry from drought,
        collapsing from my knees. I should show myself. I should
ask what happened. Crying. Lord, the crying. I cannot live
        in this place. Someone will call. Someone will end up alive.

THE AUTHOR AS MAN WHO SEES DARK ANNIE DISAPPEAR INTO THE DARKNESS BEFORE HER THROAT'S SLIT BY JACK THE RIPPER IN *FROM HELL*

After the film by Albert and Allen Hughes

On the day the rain finally stopped, I could breathe again,
        a blanket you could see through draped over me, when
we learned—those of us ignored, kicked, tripped over—
        that life, what's left now, is nothing to anyone, the lives
that Abberline couldn't save. Some of us were witnesses that week:
        averting our eyes, hearing the slices & methodical cuts,
wishing we could be heroes, since dying is laughable for us now.
        But we never stirred & left ourselves under the fog & lamps
to listen & always remember what we heard. Always grapes
        they mentioned, grapes that won't be the delicacy they are
in the future, & Laudanum, the combination they wanted,
        that Dark Annie needed as she walked into the corridor
& slowly disappeared into the night, the carriage blocking my view
        before I waited for a scream, a breath, & heard nothing.

THE AUTHOR AS MAN WHO'S WALKING DOWN THE STREET AS FRANKIE FLOWERS GETS SHOT THROUGH THE CHEST IN THE PUBLIC PARKING LOT IN *TRAFFIC*

After the film by Steven Soderbergh

I wanted to leave & made bad excuses & did everything
        I could to hide away from the life I never wanted & have
to live with now: smog & traffic & routine that could be
        replaced with any other words, nothing I ever predicted
for my future. At first I thought squibs & blanks, but no
        streets were blocked off & no cameras & trucks & trailers
were taking up spaces in the parking lot. Then the screams
        & more shots & guns drawn. I ran to the opposite corner
& ducked into a cafe. A minute later the car exploded
        & everyone stared at each other, not admitting in words
our happiness to be safe & hope that it wouldn't spill
        into everything behind closed doors. All of it told me then
that if I needed something more, I had it. That if I wanted
        something beyond guilt, this place could always present it.

THE AUTHOR AS MAN WHO'S WALKING BY THE SIDE OF THE ROAD WHILE THE BUS PLUMMETS INTO THE RIVER IN *THE SWEET HEREAFTER*

After the film by Atom Egoyan

You think the weight would sling the bus: back
　　　　slamming the front forward, some bright, reverse
catapult on the thinner part of the ice, latticed thicker
　　　　& outward, a center untouched by those children,
who were too young to understand fear, unable to know
　　　　about blades that slice through seats, the strength
to just crack a window—with water cold enough
　　　　for hypothermia, cold enough for breaths to choke
without getting air. I watched them, watched the bus
　　　　slowly disappear without fire, explosion, black plumes
rippling the frozen roots upon the lower banks. I knew
　　　　that I could do nothing, thought of a small obituary,
no mug shot, how I'd never become a hero—all among
　　　　the cries I never heard, & want to, & never will.

The Author as Physics Teacher Who Witnesses Joey Get Shot by Machine Gun Fire on the Front Steps of the Regis School in *Toy Soldiers*

After the film by Daniel Petrie Jr.

I've asked for little, I swear to you: my health, students
     who hope for success, a family. In any way that matters.
Forced into random rooms: to sleep is a thing of the past.
     Work & vectors & projectiles: as in bullets, as in Joey
on the steps & screaming, someone who'd be standing
     here no longer. We watched his face. We watched
his body writhe & contort, & the first thing I thought of
     was each angle: telling me I've failed in this life, failed
to understand how oceans are swallowing islands, how
     I should've been up there with him, shots to the stomach
& the gun still firing, as his limbs lost control & he fell
     like a punching bag: limp & devoid of anything we calculate.
What I ask for is it to end, & quickly. What I beg for is his eyes
     to be closed when zipped, when dragged, when leaving.

THE AUTHOR AS WEDDING GUEST WHO SEES THE BRIDE ON THE ROOF BEFORE SHE COMMITS SUICIDE BY FREE FALLING FROM THE LEDGE IN *THE DEVIL'S DOUBLE*

After the film by Lee Tamahori

There was nothing that could ruin the day: only
    the heat that we were all used to, & the dry air
that our lungs accepted after too many years.
    I remember their smiles, how they looked happy,
before I saw Uday & the look in his eyes, raising
    his glasses to stare & lick his lips. I'd only met him
in passing & immediately turned away, then watched
    as he moved toward her, the groom walking behind,
& I don't know how much time passed before
    I looked up & saw her: some ethereal afterglow
instead of a woman who was just married & had
    everything in front of her. She crashed into the table
right next to mine: blood staining her dress, eyes
    toward the sun, the last thing she saw his body on hers.

THE AUTHOR AS MAN WHO, FROM THE OPPOSITE CORNER OF THE STREET, SEES SANDRA GET SHOT THROUGH THE NECK IN *BLITZ*

After the film by Elliott Lester

That week the rain wouldn't stop, pooled & flooded
        the sewers, & even with the windows closed, the barrage
was like blood pulsing through the heart, never ceasing.
        I was walking the opposite way, saw him closing on her
in all black, an oversized hood shrouding his face, before
        she stopped & one shot went through her neck. I ducked
behind a van, could barely see as the rain came down harder,
        before the blood flowed, black amidst the shadows
as she gasped & choked for air. I knew she was gone,
        but called & blurted out words: *Hurt. Hurry. Now. Can't.*
I don't know if mine was the last face she saw, or she knew
        if my eyes looked directly into hers. They said they'd come.
I snapped my phone in two, threw it down a sewer,
        & always imagine I could've done something more.

The Author as Man Who's Walking a Few Blocks from the Bank During the Robbery in Progress in *Heat*

After the film by Michael Mann

What I could do was cower behind a bench, their guns
        still firing, as women—far away but never far enough
from the one second & trajectory & fortuity that could
        end an existence—still ran, holding onto children
in their arms. & as others looked in all directions, I felt
        I had to question my own exit that morning, & if I still
was alive. Two men turned a corner before more cops
        followed in the same direction, sirens echoing between
the buildings & alleys, & still I felt safer there, behind
        anything, instead of being out in the open, which I was
in the end, no matter what. Someone shot stumbled
        around the corner in the distance, choked unheard
words to God, hand on their chest, as I strained to hear
        footsteps, bullets through metal, far & forgotten voices.

THE AUTHOR AS NEIGHBOR WHO HEARS THE GUNSHOT AND LOOKS THROUGH HIS WINDOW TO SEE WILSON RUSHING OUT OF THE HOUSE AND SCREAMING IN *LOVE LIZA*

After the film by Todd Louiso

It was dawn, we were barely awake, & light shattered
      through the blinds: a blanket we'd draped to shroud
ourselves into sleep again, which didn't work. His voice
      first before the screams, & I jumped, left you there
to turn in bed, as if you heard nothing. We never knew them,
      & for years lived just yards from each other. I watched
through our bathroom window, wondered if I should call 911
      or wait until he did—I didn't know if it was my place
or what happened. She pulled it in their guest bedroom,
      we found out days later, & left no note. What could we say?
There was a van & cleaning crew. But this happens. We just
      never thought so close to our home. Three weeks later,
after he torched his house, we felt our own bodies on fire,
      & promised to move soon, to never speak of it again.

The Author as Anonymous Computer Student Looking Back Years Later in *Capturing the Friedmans*

After the documentary film by Andrew Jarecki

One of many, & for that you can call me anything, since
        nothing can be proven. There were black screens & dull
green flashes, the off-white heaviness of monitors like chains
        wrapped around wrists, always stretching. Mathematics
defined by wood paneling, black lines I counted before
        I always looked into his eyes, saw sweat on his forehead,
knew only later about the magazine cache. But what man
        doesn't have his secrets? In every episode of *To Catch
a Predator* we see, feigned or not, some sense of sorrow
        in their eyes, & never will we know what, if anything,
they'd have done. There was no fantasy lived in my class,
        in that basement, no games of leapfrog played: just dust
& the stench of unwashed hair, the faint aroma of singed
        electrical wires, sparks set to catch. But nothing ever did.

THE AUTHOR AS NEIGHBOR WHO SEES TOM POUNDING ON THE MCCARTHY'S FRONT DOOR AFTER ADAM SHOOTS HIMSELF IN *STIR OF ECHOES*

After the film by David Koepp

We talked every week, it seemed then, about needing
        to move: crack dealers on corners near dawn, cars
on blocks soon after dusk. Everything that somehow
        avoided us. But that morning you drove off to Joliet
to visit your sister, I could tell no one about the shot
        I heard: staring through the curtains, wondering if
it was only a firecracker, then knowing it wasn't. You knew
        we didn't belong: never going to football games, never
going to block parties—only driving to our jobs, trying
        to save enough to eventually leave for somewhere far
from all we predicted. But Tom was there, somehow
        instantly, screaming & pounding on the door, & through
the window I wondered: *Frank? Adam?* I knew Tom knew
        who it was, & could only stare at their painting on the wall.

THE AUTHOR AS LANDLORD WHO FINDS MAJID'S BODY AN HOUR AFTER HE'S SLIT HIS THROAT IN *CACHÉ*

After the film by Michael Haneke

Lord, the blood. There is no blessing for this. Black
        is the color, & the gasoline I smell with this ending—
exhaust, colorless, billowing in, the one curtain limp
        & convulsing after seconds. I saw him rarely, slow walk
out the door, his face saying nothing. If what I can sense
        tells me I'm alive, I don't know what I would choose.
The blade fell from his hand. Blood scythes the jambs.
        They say not to touch anything, & with a towel over
my face, who to call first? No one can know about
        closed doors. No one will know what happened here.
If we believe the movies: his ghost wavered, wrenched
        from his body, plans never to be made, & maybe
a son to make decisions, to come up with money, time
        for something proper, some incessant new beginning.

THE AUTHOR AS MAN CLIMBING RECREATIONALLY WHO'S UNSEEN ACROSS THE CANYON AS HE WITNESSES THE AVALANCHE IN *CLIFFHANGER*

After the film by Renny Harlin

Because the snow is falling, because I am here & falling
     & listening, I see them, early, too early, before the man
takes the plunge from the mountain's edge. I hear gunfire
     before the avalanche, before I hope no one knows I'm here.
There's just air now, & snow, the failing to not look down
     while, hooked in, I can't do anymore. Dear God,
I've given you nothing & I know this. Keep me safe. Shatter me
     like stars, like light through a hailstorm, & I'll hold on.
The guns fire & I wait, wait for them to see me here—blood-ripe
     knuckles gripped—for everyone there to spot me, cowering
in some kind of prayer, for stability, a pausing of spent muscles
     & life to hand me the pass to be afraid now. Because I am.
& I've always been. The snow keeps falling & I'm safe again
     among this foothold, this slipping, this peace now.

THE AUTHOR AS NEIGHBOR WHO SEES COURTNEY SHOOT HERSELF IN THE HEAD FROM HIS LIVING ROOM WINDOW ACROSS THE STREET IN *BELLFLOWER*

After the film by Evan Glodell

My youth? I hear it mostly in the revved engines & tires
          squealing, shattered beer bottles & cursing, & somehow
admire it, live through them now, the only neighbor,
          I imagine, who hasn't called the cops. & to see it then
& ask what happened, as if there's some explanation
          that would make me sleep without seeing her scream
his name before the quickness of the barrel to her head
          & the shot & slowing of time as her body collapses
in the street & he keeps walking. Then was my time to call,
          but I couldn't get away from the window, where
anyone could see me if they looked. But no one did.
          I turned the lights off, hid in my bedroom for days,
ignored their knocks. I couldn't relive it. I couldn't say
          what I saw tells us the world won't wait much longer.

THE AUTHOR AS MAN WHO SEES THE WOMAN SHOT DIRECTLY IN THE BACK AS SECURITY STARTS SHOOTING INTO THE CROWD IN *THE RUNNING MAN*

After the film by Paul Michael Glaser

2017: a year I never thought I'd see, & still I may not
        as I crouch, the woman twenty feet ahead, two bullets
directly into her back. We all knew it would come to this:
        no gasoline & hurricanes, contraband & earthquakes, all of it
we kept hidden in our closets, under beds, songs we've left
        in our heads, slowly forgotten since music's been banned,
since everyone chose to keep other memories. The doors
        rush open & everyone's escaping now. I made the decision,
the wrong one, to duck & hide from it, waiting for cold steel
        pressed against my head. But soon the screams stop. Just neon
lights in the background, this ridiculous set, all of us cheering on
        the stalkers: decapitations, unbearable volts of electricity,
chainsaws severing legs. We're all used to this now. All of us.
        & if I make it through the fire, what will be left of this life?

The Author as Man Who Runs with the Others as They Start Turning into Clothes in *War of the Worlds*

After the film by Steven Spielberg

There's no explanation for this: I started running before
          everyone else, got the head start I hoped would save
my life, before flesh turned to vapor & their clothes
          floated to the ground like all the snow & ash surrounding
everything. But we ran, & I don't know who made it out
          alive. Somehow I turned a corner, found a basement
in a diner, covered my ears & shut my eyes. There was fire
          & rubble & smoke from the left-on burners above, alarms
ringing in the distance. In that way, I knew: it would be better
          to burn alive than to go the way of the others. I waited.
It happened fast. No one else was with me. At some point
          I thought I was gone, but knew that, somehow, across
the state, you found better shelter. I didn't know how long
          I should wait, if what happened to us was just beginning.

What We Ask for Can Never Be Granted

THE AUTHOR AS MAN WHO THINKS HE WON'T MAKE IT OUT OF THE PARTY ALIVE AFTER SEEING TONY'S BODY IN THE ELEVATOR IN *DIE HARD*

After the film by John McTiernan

What I can ask for now: an apology I can give you
        if I ever leave this floor, which I imagine I won't
as I stare into his open eyes, blank face, the Santa hat
        resting there silently, all before the screams start
& I wonder if my heart would stop if I escaped
        & was able to jump, if it would seize in the middle
of the fall. Things don't happen like this. People
        usually don't escape—so why should we? I thought
about prayer as I stared at my father in the casket
        & how I was never able to recite one: not in the time
he was dying, an entire year with the help of machines,
        or even when he was alive. I don't know what they want,
but if the building goes up in flames, let me not be
        trapped, unable to move, & let it end before it begins.

The Author as Man Who Finally Believes After He Sees Half of the Biker's Body Dragged Back by the Rope in *The Mist*

After the film by Frank Darabont

Still in the background, I watched & waited & spoke
       a prayer I kept silent, one that—after the shroud of mist
suffocated the air & formed into white nests of blindness—
       served no purpose, as we watched his legs get dragged
& the rope slick with his blood. I knew then, an hour
       after you sent me to get tomato sauce & two bottles
of cheap Malbec, that I probably wouldn't come back.
       But even more than that, I wondered if I was luckier
than you, & if the mist came through the small cracks
       in our windows, those I never called the landlord about
after your constant reminders. No one's cell phone works
       now. No one has faith we'll survive. The first sign
of darkness is almost here, & we have nothing left to do
       but wait, think of a plan, & ask if we'll ever see morning.

THE AUTHOR AS MAN WHO WATCHES THE FUNERAL PROCESSION OF COCOONED BODIES FROM HIS SECOND STORY APARTMENT WINDOW IN *KILLER KLOWNS FROM OUTER SPACE*

After the film by Stephen Chiodo

Reports on the radio & news stories. Nothing we believed,
      & weeks since I saw you, your plane on its flight across
the country, when we said next time those weeks would
      never pass. They were horrific, walked slowly down our street,
& still I thought: *Some prank*, before their guns spit webs
      of pink & bodies turned to cocoons, before the man bolted
& didn't make it alive, lifeless & bouncing near the truck
      that sped away, before I wanted to scream for them
to find you, since I knew then I could not be saved. But I waited
      in the dark, my face hidden in the black, & watched
as they vacuumed & collected, piles & piles on rainbow sleds,
      & listened for a knock, feet busting down the door.
But nothing came. I was there for hours, fell asleep until
      dawn: party streamers & confetti still littering the alleys.

The Author as Man Who Watches from His Attic Window During the Decapitation in *Hobo with a Shotgun*

After the film by Jason Eisener

In this Technicolor city: graffiti, the stench from sewers,
      hookers on every corner. The way I always said it would be.
Boards & black bars over my windows, except the highest one,
      where I watched the gang leader from my attic, clearing mice
that suffocated & couldn't escape. I watched his son drive away,
      barbed wire ripping cleanly through the man's neck—
blood spurting like twenty squibs went off, the movie prop
      no one can get to look real. It always happened like this: hidden
or out in the open, you could watch, as long as no challenge
      was heard & no words were spoken. & for years now no one
has bothered me—I have nothing anyone would want. Still, when
      you left me those years ago, I thought I'd eventually escape,
find some place in the country, show you that I could forgive
      & that somehow, away from this city, I'm still alive & well.

THE AUTHOR AS MAN WHO, THROUGH BINOCULARS, SEES SHERIFF BOYD SHOT AND DYING ON THE SIDE OF THE ROAD IN *BREAKDOWN*

After the film by Jonathan Mostow

This life that's taken its toll, & this place I'll never leave
        that I always told myself I would. A long walk in the heat,
winding roads & rocks & hills: anything to take me out
        of my mind, the way you left me, how I did nothing
to stop you or the moving truck that I thought I could see
        for an endless stretch of miles. Through them: the cruiser
& gunshots & the man tripping over the edge & nothing
        I could do to help or stop it. The cop was shot & I swore
I could hear static among the dust, then the man in black
        who fell in slow motion. I waited. An hour later, too late:
an ambulance & two men being loaded into it. What could
        I tell them? Once dusk settled & the sky turned pink
to black, I knew I'd witnessed something I wanted
        to write you in a letter, if you'd ever believe me again.

The Author as Man Who Watches the Bites and Strangulations from His Seat in *Snakes on a Plane*

After the film by David R. Ellis

Because this is my world now: the screaming, blue faces,
        open mouths of every living thing. I was afraid of those
small, colorless, harmless: as they slithered through dirt
        & under azalea bushes, or the black rat snakes in woods
blending with dank skunk cabbage & dead leaves. I can
        only watch now, paralyzed, rows of hazard lights glowing
on the aisle sides, no way to save anyone as I crouch near
        an emergency exit, rattle the handle, thinking I can jump
not to save myself, but to avoid dying slowly from venom,
        not have my breath taken by the coiled ease of predator
on prey. Bullets start to fly. Frantic shakes of my shoulders
        to no avail—I won't look up, & then I think of you, how
when you read about this, you won't believe it, the luck of it all,
        & that if I make it out alive, you'll forgive me for everything.

THE AUTHOR AS MAN WHO'S ON THE ESCALATOR DUCKING FROM BULLETS AS QUAID USES A DEAD BODY FOR A SHIELD IN *TOTAL RECALL*

After the film by Paul Verhoeven

The love I felt for each breath upon my neck was limitless—
    a new woman every week, every morning. Dear God,
I've prayed, but the bullets are sprayed & tangential: everywhere.
    I wonder, now, always, about my life that will end here—
a life where it's just me, trapped, trampled, & endless. Endless
    but beginning: the way the world tells us we've been good
to each other, or that we matter in the end. I hope to leave
    here, & hear nothing but silence, or wind, but the bullets
are flying with the screams & the bodies, & I'm here now
    among them all. I look, for one second, & see blood across
the escalators: limbs flailing, never knowing who's alive. I hope
    to tell you this. & this is it, I think—I think we're done for.
But it's just me. & if I don't make it out, know that you didn't
    deserve the life you had. It was me until the end, & it's over.

THE AUTHOR AS MAN WHO STARES OUT HIS WINDOW ACROSS THE STREET TO SEE THE AMBULANCE CRASH AND THE WEREWOLF KILL THE DRIVER IN *THE MONSTER SQUAD*

After the film by Fred Dekker

What I asked for when you left: to never contact me
        again, to take everything, to leave me here & pack
your bags, & you obliged. & even after it all, when I saw
        the oak nearly split in half, the growl & bites & teeth
into his neck, I couldn't think to tell anyone but you.

        His screams lasted seconds & I thought the eyes, glowing
off the full moon, looked into mine, but it happened fast:
        so fast that he took off & I watched him sprint to God
knows where. The wheels still spun on the ambulance.

        Smoke rose from the hood before flames started
from a breath into wildfire. The phone was in my hand.

        I knew he was dead & dialed your number. It rang & rang
& I stared at what I thought to be a sign that the world,
        beyond faith & luck, didn't stand a chance to survive.

The Author as Police Officer Who Thinks He's Safe Until the Detonator Goes Off in the Cyberdyne Systems Building in *Terminator 2: Judgment Day*

After the film by James Cameron

I never saw so much fire: after the bullets & our cars
        upended, when the core of the building imploded & stars
of flame like small comets flung toward us as we watched
        from behind the barrier that we knew wouldn't hold us
much longer. All those times you asked me to consider
        at least a different county, & we could move, because
something bad was about to happen. I didn't believe you
        & still think it's my only regret: your feigned sense
of knowing that not the entire world was coming to an end,
        but our world & the world of our daughter who you said
I didn't see enough, how she'd always be sleeping when
        you heard the lock turn & the open door like my breath
on your neck. I closed my eyes, was dragged further away,
        & thought I'd be lucky to have one more chance to see you.

THE AUTHOR AS MAN WHO'S SECRETLY SEEING DOLORES AND FINDS HER ON THE FLOOR IN HER APARTMENT BEFORE JUDAH IN *CRIMES AND MISDEMEANORS*

After the film by Woody Allen

It shouldn't have been me: finding the door unlocked
        after the phone kept ringing, after buzzing & sneaking in
& knocking, knowing she was waiting for him, to tell him
        it was over. I'd hoped for my mind to spiral into something
creative with the details: how she'd be sleeping, wall unit
        buzzing raucously, drowning out even knuckles over & over
on the door, & how I'd climb in with her & she'd turn over,
        only half-awake, & smile in a trance that I wanted to hold
onto forever. But her body stuck out from the foot
        of the bed, the maroon of her blouse the color of blood
from her neck. I opened the door & peeked out, wondering
        if he did it: how she was truly going to tell his wife, & then
walked away, closing the door, thinking how cops would ask
        questions, & what would happen if I couldn't say his name.

The Author as Man Who's Walking Late Near the River as He Sees Kazanian Getting Attacked by Rats in *Inferno*

After the film by Dario Argento

The rare night in the city when you can hear yourself
        think: all that helped me not fall asleep after three days,
when I came back to find a few boxes, kitchen table
        without chairs, & your key right inside the door
to tell me I'd done everything wrong. I can't deny
        the fleeting hope that someone would end it, & asked
if in days or weeks or months I could really move on,
        as I diverged by a river where I saw him in the distance
from office lights off the skyscrapers, falling, converging
        into awful recognition of what I thought to be a dream
before rats started gnawing at his face & legs. *They're eating*
        me alive & his words singing through the alleys of the city
to no avail, as I rubbed my eyes & looked away & asked
        if it was a prediction, for my life, of what was to come.

THE AUTHOR AS STUDENT WHO HAS A CRUSH ON TINA AND WATCHES OUTSIDE HER WINDOW AS SHE'S MURDERED BY FREDDY IN *A NIGHTMARE ON ELM STREET*

After the film by Wes Craven

Tina, the love I had was inexpressible, but what I thought
        I could keep always in my head—no letters, no diary,
no paintings—could not last forever. Not once did I see him,
        because I never told you. I told no one. That night I was there,
saw Rod screaming, his back wrenched, almost snapping
        the walls. When he shattered lamps & bulbs, I looked away
from the blood, squinted to see anything, then took off across
        the lawns. It was too early that morning, & my parents
would wake too soon. There was the smell of cut grass
        & gasoline. My heart felt like it would explode. I crept
to my room, waited for the footsteps of my father. I read
        the headlines in the papers. I knew. Days later I saw words
of Rod's suicide. I knew. & now that I've fallen in love again,
        I can speak of this, still knowing, & never say a word.

THE AUTHOR AS MAN WHO ESCAPES FROM THE SECRET MEETING AS HE SEES THE OTHERS SHOT BY THE COPS IN *THEY LIVE*

After the film by John Carpenter

How it got to this point—wishful thinking, overthrow,
      a world we could conquer—I still don't know. I came
because there was work. We all did. Our families still
      thousands of miles away. We agreed that something
had to be done. The last meeting: new people, contacts,
      weapons laid out like Sunday brunch. Some of them
were humans, & it was only a matter of time before
      it didn't matter, before none of us were left alive.
I heard Frank say: *We'll do anything to be rich*, & before
      I escaped through the back door, saw ten rounds
rip through his chest, I asked myself if everything
      was worth it, if upon my return you'd have another
lover, live in another state, tell our children my time
      ran out, & in the morning take them away for good.

The Author as Man Who Sees Students Climbing Out of Windows of the High School from Across the Street in *Elephant*

After the film by Gus Van Sant

I thought I was dreaming at first, heard the faint pops
        & screams through open windows: track or gym class
or commands at the flag girls. But after being here
        for almost five years, nothing came together like this,
from the smoke I saw—staring out our bedroom window—
        to the kids running, all of them away from the school.
The funnel cloud shifted over the roof, & I rubbed
        my eyes until I could only see black, but it was spreading
& didn't fade. You rolled over & I left you there, curls
        I joked reminded me of Medusa the only part of you
I could see. I asked the question: *Why here?* & had nothing
        I could say in return, but wanted to believe that it wasn't
what I knew, wasn't what we'd read about, all before
        our plan to move, as if we'd ever, just us, be in any danger.

THE AUTHOR AS MAN WHO SEES LISA GET SHOT IN THE HEAD AT THE MINI-MART FROM HIS CAR BEFORE THE ROBBER TAKES OFF INTO THE NIGHT IN *PASSENGER 57*

After the film by Kevin Hooks

Already drunk & you asking for more, I abide & drive
      to the place we avoid, one with a robbery, it seems,
almost every week, something we feel guilty for, something
      we wish wasn't true. Outside, the car running, I smoke
my last cigarette, remember you saying: *Cheap*. I never
      thought we'd end up like this, & God knows there has
to be a reason why we're still in love. Ashing it, smoke
      rising, I see him go in, the guy behind the counter duck,
& without a mask, a gun drawn. I can only watch: the one
      in the back, empty, mouthed words, hands waving, metal
now to her head as he pleads nothing I can understand.
      One shot & she drops. & I duck, waiting for him to see
the exhaust, the last wisp of smoke, when there's nothing left
      but him cradling her head, & her open eyes toward his.

THE AUTHOR AS MAN WHO'S ECLIPSED BY THE DARK UNDER THE OPPOSITE SIDE OF THE BRIDGE AND SEES THE CAR PLUNGE INTO THE RIVER IN *BLOW OUT*

After the film by Brian De Palma

By the time I got there, I knew you'd crossed the state
       into Ohio, & the time you needed would stretch past
a week into a month before a year, before you'd decide
       to have me box everything, leave, give you a time
I wouldn't be there to collect every one, & drive away
       for good. I needed water then, a belief in consistence,
in directions that change with the weather & clouds
       fading into the black, starless sky. It was above me before
I thought it was teenagers, before I saw the car suddenly skid
       into the water, & froze, then watched the frame of a man
on the other side & another man dive in: the whole time
       thinking I was alone. I wondered—if I'd had the chance
before him—if it could've been me: a headline & photo
       just one state away, all to show you I could begin again.

What We Hope Will Never Find Us

THE AUTHOR AS MAN WHO, WHILE JOGGING ON THE BEACH, SEES ANOTHER MAN GETTING STRANGLED BY PIANO WIRE IN THE DISTANCE IN *MANIAC*

After the film by William Lustig

An early run & the chill that makes even your tendons feel
       draped with ice, as if one more breath & your heart
will stop—no one walking the beach, the coroner finally there
       one day later, three others loading you into a black hearse
fifty yards away. I'm used to seeing no one: the time each bar
       sounds last call, sun slowly ascending over the Hudson. Now,
half a mile away, a man moving toward the dunes, scrub wood
       collected in his arms, magic hour turning still to morning.
Then someone behind him & I stop, my throat caught—
       his legs off the sand & neck being strangled as I kneel,
crawl closer to a dune, dying beach grass doing nothing
       to hide me from view. But they're too far away & he's fast—
two bodies loaded into his car & slowly driving away. I'll call
       from a payphone, leave no name: only what I think I saw.

THE AUTHOR AS MAN WHO WATCHES SAM GET MURDERED FROM A DARK ALLEY AND PROCEEDS TO HIDE AS HE LISTENS TO MOLLY SCREAM IN *GHOST*

After the film by Jerry Zucker

I was there, among the stench & decay & back alleys—
        beyond the filth of this place. I was waiting to score
from a no-show, & saw the guy come from nowhere,
        some dark street at a distance. I can make it all up
with excuses & inexcusables, but it wouldn't work
        for this. I watched & watched. I heard her scream, & thought
maybe he wasn't dead, that the gods, & luck, somehow, saved
        a life that night, & I was witness to it: to heaven, to love,
to the world of screaming & dying ghosts. Because
        that's what we get in the end: the fearlessness, & the fear
of a watcher who feels for his life, & knows he can do it all
        but walk over, after, & offer some condolence, something
to say this will all work out. & we hope it will, since we know
        those dark alleys are places we need, we feel, & end with.

THE AUTHOR AS MAN WHO WATCHES THE LAKE SHORE STRANGLER TRY TO ESCAPE AS GUNSHOTS RING OUT IN *CHILD'S PLAY*

After the film by Tom Holland

I shouldn't have, but I followed them: among the neon
        of Chinese restaurants, peep shows, the blinding prism
of the toy store, lit up 24 hours a day. To duck & hide
        behind cars, telephone poles, alley garbage cans: it worked.
Neither saw me. For months we followed the news, learned
        to look for his weapons, locked our doors at dusk, never
knowing where or who he'd strike next. *I got the strangler*
        was all I needed to hear: shot after shot, each windshield
shattered, glass twinkling on the black streets. I hid behind
        a Camaro as they each stumbled in: neon almost blinding
as it reflected off the rain, the screams & shots & trails
        of blood before the lightning, as I watched the explosion,
otherworldly on this cold Chicago night, & waited for my life
        to have some meaning, something no one saw but me.

THE AUTHOR AS MAN WHO'S HIDING IN THE DARK STREET CORNER AS FALLON SHOOTS TEDDY AT POINT-BLANK RANGE IN *JUDGMENT NIGHT*

After the film by Stephen Hopkins

Always cold & dark: these nights of no civilians passing,
      only those of us with hands over makeshift fires, holes
even in the drums, warmth exiting every chance it gets—
      the only light other than cops passing, not one ever braking,
even on a night like this, the RV threaded between alley walls,
      smoke rising in silence, where I retreated from the heat
& lone streetlight above. Soon he was surrounded by guns
      & echoing voices, as I waited for the shot, blood to pour
from the back of his head. I would've been killed on sight,
      but I was hidden in the back corner of the street, watched
his back twist slowly, falling until still, before flames & shots
      & everyone running. They left him there, didn't throw him
into some dumpster, as if this part of the city houses each one—
      eyes pecked away by vultures, faces glaring toward magic hour.

THE AUTHOR AS MAN WHO, WHILE OUT WALKING AT NIGHT, SEES ABIN COOPER SHOOT DEPUTY PETE IN THE CHEST WITH A SHOTGUN IN *RED STATE*

After the film by Kevin Smith

Always the stories of walks without you: birds chirping
        in barren, leafless trees, distant factories & pneumatic
doors, drills echoing off the sides of massive buildings—
all replaced, now, by the blast I hear, & diving behind
a stump newly wrenched from the ground, from the storm
        that swept through this city just one day ago. I didn't know
if I was next then, if someone glaring through the windows
        would call out to eliminate the witness. For the last year
the only sounds that came from their property were swells
        of notes off the organ pipes, curling & fading into the air
like your breath in the cold on the day you left. He lied there
        until they decided to move the body, find a way to hide
the police car. I ran when I had my chance, looked over
        my shoulder, & waited for footsteps I knew would come.

THE AUTHOR AS MAN WHO RUNS WITH THE OTHERS AS THEY TRY TO ESCAPE FROM THE MONSTER IN *THE HOST*

After the film by Joon-ho Bong

Like everyone else, I see it: first formless, then coiling
        its tail around rafters under the bridge, swinging
before diving, before it runs up & down the concrete
        to attack, & I'm one too who stares at the painted trailer,
the locked door, hands trying to push their way through—
        before the slaughter, the blood on their faces & arms,
& I wonder what to do but run, as I'm behind it now,
        watching it finally take the girl, her father screaming, chasing
after it with others, while I go the opposite direction, crawl
        under a bus in the parking lot, unable to hear anything
but the roar coupled with screams, feet still pounding
        the cement before followers do the same, saving
ourselves, not able to say we're doing it to go home to the one
        we don't deserve, the one we really want to live for.

THE AUTHOR AS MAN WHO STARES OUT HIS WINDOW WITH THE OTHERS AS JOHN ROONEY AND HIS MEN ARE GUNNED DOWN IN THE STREET IN *ROAD TO PERDITION*

After the film by Sam Mendes

What we want can be provided, if only we wait, & wait
   for what we never deserved, like the sound of bullets
cascading off bricks in this alley, & not of bullets,
   but the echo between buildings, as I imagine all of us
watching, curtains drawn, each man methodically
   writhing, forefinger on the trigger, nothing spoken
from anyone: watching, shooting, falling. To have faith
   is a wash these days: we know this. To look & see
each man falling is what my nightmares brought
   to my home, my wife, my children, & everyone else
staring out their window then: in this, never away
   from this, never away from trying to find something
miles down the road, in another state, another country,
   another place where we understand little of all we see.

THE AUTHOR AS MAN WHO SEES THE DOCTOR GET SUCKED INTO THE EARTH AND HIS WIFE SUCCUMB TO THE SAME FATE IN THE STATION WAGON SOON AFTER IN *TREMORS*

After the film by Ron Underwood

At this hour, nothing but dust coating the lungs no matter
      how you try to escape, so I sit here watching—six pack
in hand—lights from their generator, & only this starless sky
      in the distance, miles of black from the peak of these rocks.
It's been days now, & I wait until dark, but they're slow,
      & I wait mainly to see when they'll fail—everyone fails
who's lived here, who's decided to settle here, in Perfection,
      away from phones, medicine, hospitals. Nothing's happened
to me, & I don't understand why. When the rumbling starts
      I barely feel it, but the vibrations shake their bodies, panic
in their eyes until the generator's pulled under, & suddenly
      so is the doctor. I stand & don't dare to run & help—
it's too steep for someone like me. I want to scream: *Get away*
      from the station wagon. & now: nothing but music & headlights.

The Author as Man Who Watches through the Trees as Bruce Gets Killed After Being Struck by the Convertible in *The Informers*

After the film by Gregor Jordan

The distant bass & howl of synths that drew me to this
        mansion: arranged with fire, sequins shattering light,
those inside shrouded by the curtain's gauze. The filter
        of the in & out: cars sleek & ever-changing, dropping off,
picking up, interminable music, the pulse louder & louder
        as night turned to morning. Opulence I never saw in the Valley.
I waited from the trees, prepared to enter too late: all so lost
        in their heads they wouldn't notice. But before I could stand,
the convertible threw him, like light speed, onto the bricks.
        There were screams before a few stood watching, before
the rest went on ignoring: some in the bathroom snorting
        their fifth line of the night, some by the pool, shallow
plunges into their veins. All before the cops, the ambulance—
        not one soul around now, sun still glinting off the water.

THE AUTHOR AS MAN WHO, WHILE FISHING FURTHER DOWN THE SWAMP, THINKS HE SEES SOMETHING MURDER SAMSON AND AINSLEY IN *HATCHET*

After the film by Adam Green

No binoculars: just a pole & bait & the boat I thought
        would never hold again. I never knew why it was illegal
& questioned the motives for it: endangered species, stories
        of Crowley & voodoo & curses, but nothing had happened,
& though I caught little, it was quiet, always quiet, even
        if that night changed it all, when I saw them from a distance,
could make out ghost lights swarming above the swamp
        before growling & voices & a sound like chopped wood
that kept me there, still & waiting. It wasn't more
        than a minute & only then did I start to believe, waiting
again for whatever it was to find me, to the point
        where even breathing made me nervous. But only after
first light I got it moving again, to witness only smudged
        photos & headlines saying it was nothing but alligators.

THE AUTHOR AS MAN SURVIVING ON THE ROOF WHO FINALLY HEARS THE MOTORCYCLE GANG DRIVE INTO THE MALL PARKING LOT AND START SHOOTING IN *DAWN OF THE DEAD*

After the film by George Romero

I'm starting to hear things: a thousand bees buzzing
          around a single chrysanthemum, helicopter blades
whirling into a crescendo of indeterminate cacophony,
          & my daughter's front-teeth-gone smile & the hose
in her hands shattering light through the sun as dusk
          makes its way into the city. All of it: a distant memory.
I stole soup cans & utensils & have survived on those—
          watching them shuffle & groan & walk in tired circles,
bumping into doors & abandoned trucks & themselves.
          Then the gang & shotguns: I was saved. But the bullets
flew & I was afraid they'd mistake me for one of them,
          or realize I couldn't help them & kill for that alone.
I ducked & listened. I waited for it to stop, for a sign
          that I could live here, finally, in this endless silence.

THE AUTHOR AS MAN WHO SEES UNCLE CHARLIE
GET SHOT THROUGH THE NECK IN *HARD RAIN*

After the film by Mikael Salomon

It wouldn't stop, & I knew this. The sheriff missed me:
   I hid in the basement. By then it would be too much trouble
to find anyone. But finally I knew I had to leave: a cheap
   inflatable in hand for this eventual emergency. The lights
from the truck were blinding: statues & telephone poles
   almost below the waterline as I waded. I heard their voices
a minute before shots were fired, & it was clearly a man,
   as if God finally appeared, glaring in the form of white light
we finally sink into. I hid behind a statue & waited. What
   could I do to help? & then the blood as it poured, as his head
lolled under, then back up, wavering. It didn't take long.
   When the lights were shot out, & the other man dragged bags
through the flood, they followed, & it was silent, before
   I found an alley through buildings, & hoped it would hold.

The Author as Man Who Finds Megan Dead in the Car by the Side of the Road in *The House of the Devil*

After the film by Ti West

To be out on Friday night metal detecting: something I'd tell
        no one, even if someone listened. It sounded like an M-80
as I scaled the hillside, sweeping through shrubs, damp ferns,
        hoping one-in-a-million would be an American Gold Eagle
someone didn't know they were tossing. The car was idle—
        exhaust seeping into formless clouds in the cold. I stopped,
looked at the black sheen on the windows & windshield,
        saw her head slack & to the side. The heat was on high,
the only sound now: a steady, rattled whoosh, & on the roads,
        no cars in sight, just her headlights still gleaming. Afraid
to touch anything, I stared, while the blood still ran silently
        down her jacket. No phone. No nearby houses. I turned
& tripped down the embankment, detector snapping,
        hoped no blood left the car: one shoeprint to lock me away

THE AUTHOR AS ADDICT WHO STUMBLES NEAR ROOM EIGHT AT THE HOTEL BROSLIN TO SEE BELIAL NEARLY RIP O'DONOVAN'S FACE OFF IN *BASKET CASE*

After the film by Frank Henenlotter

These days there's nothing to live for: peep shows, bars
      open until sunrise, forgetting to eat: all of it too easy, & you
can survive on almost nothing. For months now I've been
      here: a room just to sleep so no one can see me, & no one
knows my name. Someone, a week ago—tourniquet above
      elbow in a back alley—told me eight was the place, something
I felt lucky to hear, even blessed, & with twenty dollars tucked
      in my pocket, it was worth it. The door was open, the only one
I could see, & when I went to knock, it was attached, clawing
      & ripping, blood streaming, screams trying to leave his mouth,
& I couldn't look away. Now: sweating, coming down, unable
      to breathe, & almost twenty blocks away, the world won't wait
for me to come back from this, & I can't be a witness. I lock
      my door, hands over my ears, & only voices: louder & louder.

THE AUTHOR AS NEIGHBOR WHO, AFTER HEARING RORY BARK FOR TOO LONG, WALKS OVER TO FIND PAM AND SALLY'S BODIES IN *IN THE LINE OF FIRE*

After the film by Wolfgang Petersen

Five minutes after the shots, after we looked at each other
      & I went quietly to lock our front door, I had to go—
something you begged me not to do as we turned the TV up
      louder & louder, nothing helping to drown it out.
I knocked twice on the screen door, the sun in my eyes
      before I could see both of them on the floor, Rory
further back by the wall, & when my vision got clearer,
      blood starting to pool around their necks & arms.
It was silent otherwise: no cars or bikes in the street
      & no one out for a walk. I didn't want to go in, risk
fingerprints, leaving any trace of myself behind, so I walked
      toward our house, ready to dial numbers, & when you
asked what I saw, why my face was so pale, I thought only
      of interviews & motives & the stretchers to arrive.

The Author as Man in the Distant Field Who Watches Mikey Get Electrocuted by the Road and Guard Rail in *The Ice Storm*

After the film by Ang Lee

It wasn't the ice or snow or wind or betrayal
        that set me in my ways: but the scored, dismal
reminiscence, the way that, in the morning, the sun
        would pass itself off as something inimitable, & holy,
& beyond repair. I watched him. I watched him slide
        & become something unlike ourselves: a purity, a love
I'd passed over years ago, my whole life, watching him—
        against the rail, my throat caught, my throat singing
some hymn to my life, to some life I used to have,
        & doing nothing for him. The wires twitched. The world
was on its axis. His body jerked & I watched. Silence
        & sparks & regret. I looked at the sizzle. *Sizzle*.
Of this world & that body. Then I looked back & saw
        nothing. There was whiteness. It was night. I was alone.

The Author as Neighbor Who Hears the Gang Attacking Paul Kersey's Wife and Daughter in the Apartment Next Door in *Death Wish*

After the film by Michael Winner

It was always quiet there: low bass from records, ice
        clinking in glasses, lovemaking behind closed doors.
I had the phone in my hands, each number pushed,
        each second changing my mind. False alarms & cops
saying I could've stopped time, the bruises, paint
        sprayed on their bodies & walls. I'll never repeat
what I heard then, & it was over in minutes before
        the voice of his wife on the phone & my hands
around my ear to the wall. Then the silence. To be
        questioned—did I have to? Could I turn off the lights
& lock my bedroom door? I only knew them in passing—
        kicking snow off shoes outside our doors—
& wonder now if I can get away, if I care enough to ask
        what happened, if I can ask for anything ever again.

THE AUTHOR AS MAN IN THE BACKGROUND WHO WATCHES THE RAPE IN THE TUNNEL IN *IRREVERSIBLE*

After the film by Gaspar Noé

Is it impossible not to start with the rape scene?
        But I won't. Instead, the sine wave sickness
& pulsations, the life-saving fire extinguisher
        like a battering ram into his face: bone & sinew,
eyeballs & muscle caving in like warm loaves
of bread. I forget how old I was when I watched
the man hidden in the phone booth in *Traces of Death*,
        slug planted directly in the head of the alleged rapist
who kidnapped his daughter, all of it in slow motion:
        the spread of head-matter like watercolor paint,
& I thought, even then, *I would do the same thing.*
        & horrifically, I think the same thing now, contemplating
God, the afterlife, courtroom-diagnosed madness,
        & the peace arriving from one gunshot: a life-ending,
seconds-long act seen by so many—archived for life
        on blurred VHS tapes. & why are we led to believe
she was pregnant? They were in love at the beginning,
        before the long red tunnel, the one bystander
who walked in, saw it like I did once, stumbling drunk—
        a woman flailing, screams from an alley near McDonalds
in a part of Savannah where I lost my footing, my wallet,
        the ability to comprehend anything but shapes—
& walked away, no one knowing that peripheral
        shadow, who we see for only seconds, was me then,
& that instead of calling the police, I placed a stool
        in my room, tied the noose, & kicked it with my heel.

Acknowledgments

The author wishes to thank the editors of the following journals, in which these poems previously appeared, sometimes in earlier versions:

Bellingham Review: "The Author as Man Who Runs with the Others as They Start Turning into Clothes in *War of the Worlds*," "The Author as Man Who Watches the Bites and Strangulations from His Seat in *Snakes on a Plane*"

Collagist: "The Author as Man Who Stares Out His Window with the Others as John Rooney and His Men are Gunned Down in the Street in *Road to Perdition*"

Connotation Press: "The Author as Man Who, While Fishing Further Down the Swamp, Thinks He Sees Something Murder Samson and Ainsley in *Hatchet*," "The Author as Man Who, from the Opposite Corner of the Street, Sees Sandra Get Shot through the Neck in *Blitz*," "The Author as Man Who Sees Uncle Charlie Get Shot through the Neck in *Hard Rain*," "The Author as Man Who Watches from His Attic Window During the Decapitation in *Hobo with a Shotgun*"

Cream City Review: "The Author as Man Who Watches the Lake Shore Strangler Try to Escape as Gunshots Ring Out in *Child's Play*," "The Author as Man Who Watches through the Trees as Bruce Gets Killed After Being Struck by the Convertible in *The Informers*"

Devil's Lake: "The Author as Man Who Sees the Mechanic Get Trapped Between the Car and the Wall in *Vacancy*"

DIAGRAM: "The Author as Man Who's Walking by the Side of the Road While the Bus Plummets into the River in *The Sweet Hereafter*"

Hayden's Ferry Review: "The Author as Landlord Who Finds Majid's Body an Hour After He's Slit His Throat in *Caché*"

Linebreak: "The Author as Man Who Watches the Funeral Procession of Cocooned Bodies from His Second Story Apartment Window in *Killer Klowns from Outer Space*"

Makeout Creek: "The Author as Man Who's on the Escalator Ducking from Bullets as Quaid Uses a Dead Body for a Shield in *Total Recall*," "The Author as Student Who Has a Crush on Tina and Watches Outside Her Window as She's Murdered by Freddy in *A Nightmare on Elm Street*"

Miracle Monocle: "The Author as Man Climbing Recreationally Who's Unseen Across the Canyon as He Witnesses the Avalanche in *Cliffhanger*," "The Author as Man Who Watches Sam Get Murdered from a Dark Alley and Proceeds to Hide as He Listens to Molly Scream in *Ghost*," "The Author as Neighbor Who Hears the Gunshot and Looks through His Window to See Wilson Rushing out of the House and Screaming in *Love Liza*"

Nimrod: "The Author as Man Who's Eclipsed by the Dark Under the Opposite Side of the Bridge and Sees the Car Plunge into the River in *Blow Out*"

Quarterly West: "The Author as Man Who Finds Megan Dead in the Car by the Side of the Road in *The House of the Devil*"

RHINO: "The Author as Man in the Distant Field Who Watches Mikey Get Electrocuted by the Road and Guard Rail in *The Ice Storm*"

Sonora Review: "The Author as Man Who Finally Believes After He Sees Half of the Biker's Body Dragged Back by the Rope in *The Mist*," "The Author as Man Who Sees Students Climbing Out of Windows of the High School from Across the Street in *Elephant*," "The Author as Neighbor Who, After Hearing Rory Bark for Too Long, Walks Over to Find Pam and Sally's Bodies in *In the Line of Fire*," "The Author as Neighbor Who Sees Tom Pounding on the McCarthy's Front Door After Adam Shoots Himself in *Stir of Echoes*"

Sou'wester: "The Author as Man Who Escapes from the Secret Meeting as He Sees the Others Shot by the Cops in *They Live*," "The Author as Neighbor Who Hears the Gang Attacking Paul Kersey's Wife and Daughter in the Apartment Next Door in *Death Wish*"

Spillway: "The Author as Man Who Stares Out His Window Across the Street to See the Ambulance Crash and the Werewolf Kill the Driver in *The Monster Squad*"

Sugar House Review: "The Author as Man Surviving on the Roof Who Finally Hears the Motorcycle Gang Drive into the Mall Parking Lot and Start Shooting in *Dawn of the Dead*," "The Author as Man Who Escapes from the Secret Meeting as He Sees the Others Shot by the Cops in *They Live*"

Superstition Review: "The Author as Man Who Sees Dark Annie Disappear into the Darkness Before Her Throat's Slit by Jack the Ripper in *From Hell*," "The Author as Man Who Sees Lisa Get Shot in the Head at the Mini-Mart from His Car Before the Robber Takes Off into the Night in *Passenger 57*," "The Author as Man Who Thinks He Won't Make It Out of the Party Alive After Seeing Tony's Body in the Elevator in *Die Hard*," "The Author as Man Who, through Binoculars, Sees Sheriff Boyd Shot and Dying on the Side of the Road in *Breakdown*"

Weave Magazine: "The Author as Man Who Runs with the Others as They Try to Escape from the Monster in *The Host*"

Thanks to the following friends and poets who provided encouragement and feedback and good vibes during the writing of these poems: Sean Thomas Dougherty, Sean Harris, Luke Johnson, Gary L. McDowell, Casey Pegram, Nicholas Reading, Nick Ripatrazone, Corey Spaley, Onur Tukel, and Joe Weil.

Thanks to Brian Barker, Jesse Lee Kercheval, and Oliver de la Paz for your time and your words.

Thanks to J.P. Dancing Bear for taking a chance on another one.

Thanks to Anne Marie and Ken Montesano for always supporting my love of film.

Keith Montesano is the author of the poetry collection *Ghost Lights* (Dream Horse Press, 2010). He recently earned his PhD in English and creative writing from Binghamton University, and currently lives in New York with his wife. Find more at www.keithmontesano.com

www.ingramcontent.com/pod-product-compliance
Lightning Source LLC
Chambersburg PA
CBHW021511090426
42739CB00007B/562